# ADAMANTINE

# ADAMANTINE

✦

*Shin Yu Pai*

For Robert Alexander
So grateful to
share the White Pine
connection & to
be part of a
community together.
with gratitude,
—Shin Yu Pai

WHITE PINE PRESS / BUFFALO, NEW YORK

Published by
White Pine Press
P.O. Box 236
Buffalo, NY 14201
www.whitepine.org

Thank you to the editors of the following publications where some of these poems
first appeared, sometimes in different versions: *Reconfigurations; Yellow River Review;
Zen Monster; Urthona; Work; Tinfish; Sentence; Pena International; Origin; !Tex!;* ping
pong; "Corps de Ballet" and "Metaphysique d'ephemera" were commissioned by the
Dallas Museum of Art; "Bamiyan" was produced as a limited edition, letterpressed
broadside from Filter Press.

 Thanks to Soul Mountain and Centrum for providing the time and
space to develop this collection of work. Thanks also to 4Culture for
supporting this project.

Gasho to Norbu Rick for reading early drafts of many of these poems.

With gratitude to my husband, Kort, for his enduring love and support.

Publication of this book was made possible, in part, with public funds from the
New York State Council on the Arts.

Cover image: Elaine Ling, *Atacama Stones*, #1, silver gelatin print, 2001.
Copyright © 2010 by Elaine Ling.

Back cover: "Pine Bark Diamonds," Japanese textile design.

Book design: JB Bryan.
Set in Frederic Goudy's Deepdene.

First Edition

ISBN 978-1-935210-18-4

Printed and bound in the United States of America.

Library of Congress Control Number: 2010925983

# Contents

"...for even the *slokas* on papyrus and bound *ola* leaves would be eaten by moths and silverfish, dissolved by rainstorms – how only stone and rock could hold one person's loss and another's beauty forever."

– *Anil's Ghost*, Michael Ondaatje

## This Is Not My Story


cereal boxes in the kitchen
cupboard nibbled through
the sudden appearance of

droppings, a mouse in
the house, her lover says
*it has a very tiny heart,*

*you need only chase*
*it until it tires;* he knows
the hearts of small creatures

having chased down a few
chickens in his youth, accustomed
to how birds wear out

easily – the human heart is
a wholly different animal,
we must sense when to give in

before the other gives up

## Blind Spot

when I turn back to stare
at the man poised at the street

crossing, long after
the light has gone green

only then do I see
the round sticker affixed

to his chest

*I am deaf and blind*
in big white letters

paling in comparison to
his outfit: the oversized purple shirt

beneath the orange safety vest
in his right hand a retracted

walking stick; the way
he doesn't move, lost

in thought, I think,
the way I lose

myself in daydreaming
dumbstruck, I am

without words when
I realize there is no other

way to communicate
but through touch &

I do not have permission

when I lay my hand
upon his arm; see him

give a start; cross
traffic, just as the red palm

begins to flash, I
place myself between

his body & the hostile line
of humming cars queuing;

when we reach the other side
he's ready for me to let go

there is just *this* practice

# I Am Not Ready to Let Go

rabbit-born, I jump into
the flame to be reborn

the dumb-hearted
dog playing fetch

in the desert dune
of 110° heat

dropped dead
from giving dāna,

I do not know
my own impermanence

here, I've come
to make this offering

it is your place
not mine to say "when"

## We Are All Our Own Mothers

(AN INVOCATION FOR GREEN TARA)

I was not born
with the mothering

bone, so it's not
the young woman

my own age
on the 48 bus

hoisting her off-
spring aloft

who trains my attention,
or catches my heart

but the face of the ruined
man in a wheelchair

strapped down to the coach,
eyes gone wide watching

his jaw grown slack until
drool leaks out the corners

of the mouth he cannot wipe himself
calling out in a language which none

of us will respond to but
which we all apprehend

## Stone Face

In Yehlio, a jagged scar
runs across the neck

of Queen's Head Rock,
a vandal's foiled plot

to fence an ancient land-
mark on the art market

scarred stone hardly bears
her royal profile,

years from now to fall like

Franconia's Great Stone
Face, the Old Man

collapsing, overnight
in a slip of rock

## Burning Monk

From the remains
of his cremation,
the monks recovered

the seat of Thich Quang Duc's
consciousness –

a bloodless protest
to awaken the heart
of the oppressor

offered
at the crossing of
Phanh Dinh Phung
                  & Le Van Duyet
doused in gasoline &
immolated by 4-meter
flames the orange-robed

arhat folded in
the stillness
of full lotus

his body withering
his crown blackening

his flesh charring
his corpse collapsing

his heart refusing to burn
his heart refusing to burn
his heart refusing to burn

At 82, Luciano Mares remembers
the night his house burned to the ground
and wonders:


## DOES A MOUSE HAVE BUDDHA NATURE?


*I had some leaves*
*burning outside,*
*so I threw it in*
*the fire, mouse*
*trap – the heat*
*loosened the glue*

incensed,
the creature ran
back towards the house
where flames lit
the curtains &
spread up from there
destroying everything

# Retort

FOR YOU GUOYING

The slow rot of bedsores
and the body's putrefaction
tissue breaking down,

your husband and children
rationalized a more dignified
end – not the slow

decomposition brought
on by aneurysm and
a bedridden state

medical treatments
totaling the sum of
a family's lifetime earnings

but death by fire

on the undertaker's table
they left you
to burn

in a coffin
fashioned from
cardboard, propane

gas powering
the crematorium
where bodies glow

at 2100 degrees Fahrenheit,
organs and soft tissue
vaporizing into air

were it not for
what saved you –
the moistness of tears –

mirrored in these eyes

## Meat Stone

in the raw material
of inorganic stone

the artist saw not
mineral but animal

strata defined by bands
of color, striated quartz

a lattice of atoms in
agate, or *chalcedon*

a fantasy of corpulence –
not the actual thing itself

but the body's carcass
carved & stewed

in its own juices

the Greek bachelor
Pygmalion longed

to breathe being into
modeled marble

no small commitment
        to life

nourishing words w/
marrow & meat,

stone skinned alive,
flesh of fatty pork

feeds gray matter
acts upon the heart

served under glass
letter for letter each

gnaw & chew of language
even the herbivore imagines

## Brassica Chinensis

at the National Palace Museum
an hour before closing
the galleries are full

with visitors who've come
to view preserved plastrons
under glass, turtle shells

incised with oracle
markings – I ask my guide
what must not be missed

*the jade cabbage,*
                    she utters

nature mort
two red katydids rest
on a three-inch tall

bok choy hewn
from a single piece
of stone, material

revered among artists
for its quality
of transparency

the young concubine
who surrendered the nephrite
carving – symbol of

a father's blessing to
his favorite child –
passed over

to increase the virtue
of an elder sister's
marriage dowry

# SOLD

the aging antiquities dealer
drops the value on his idol

of the Nataraja after twenty
years, sold to the lowest

bidder for 2.4 million
insuring the collector's

early retirement – Chola bronze
buried deep within a well

bears the scars of rope
used to lower the god

down a tunnel to safety
evading all problems

of patrimony, in other
incarnations Shiva as

lingam, father of yoga
balanced in *ananda tandava*

one leg raised in cosmic dance
the other crushing illusion

## Footprint

the sledge-hammered crown
of Akshobya stolen

from Shentong Monastery's
Four Gate Pagoda,

his throat slit with saw

(if you meet the Buddha
on the path, kill him)

bought on the black market

by devotees, & donated to
the head of the Dharma Drum order

Master Sheng Yen sees
past the icon, a non-

attachment to form:
animal skin stretched over

hollow shell, a head
broken away from its body

remembering how the holy
prince was once pictured

in ancient art –
by his footprint alone

the grounding of
the transcendent

where the Buddha touched
earth, villages he visited

the dharma's spread to
distant places, Sheng Yen

retraces the path, taking
the Buddha back to his origins

from plane to bus
escorted from Beijing
to Shandong Province

a ceremony that makes
headlines on both sides

of the Taiwan Strait

## Bamiyan

in the pink sandstone cliffs
of the Koh-e Baba Mountains,

spent rocket casings,
steel support rods &

shrapnel surround a pair
of yawning outlines

carved from rock, cave
murals coated in dust &

soot, a spray-painted phrase
from the sacred Koran:

*the just replaces the unjust*

assailed by artillery
& heavy cannon fire,

faces hacked off,
then dynamited under

Talib rule &
yet it remains: nothing

*can't* be blown up

## Blossoms from a Japanese Garden

I find the gutted tome resting
on a crowded shelf between

children's books, next to
bins of printed ephemera

the illuminated pages have
been torn out clean

sheet by sheet, leaving
only a crumbled spine

a handful of poems
a table of contents,

dissatisfied, I thumb thru
stacks, find each blossom

plastic-wrapped and marked
up to twelve dollars a page

*my neighbor's bamboo*

*the fadeless flowers*

*what they saw in the moon*

watercolor sketches
by unknown artists

match each art plate
in the visual index,

the moniker Fennollosa
as foreign in these parts

as the names of Kazuko
Jiro, or Taro – characters

from the simple tales that
the curator's wife put down

in poorly rhymed verse

at cashout I argue with
the proprietor for the book

as art object, cultural document,

specimens to be studied together
                    in the garden of the reader

## Exposition

In a documentary on the Yellow River, the filmmaker charts
progress, mapping changes shaped by Three Gorges Dam


follows "Jerry" Bo Yu Chen & "Cindy" Yu Shui

       working-class laborers in China's hospitality industry,

          pleasure-boat tours of Old China catering
                    to Westerners

Jerry & Cindy parroting, "It's my pleasure."


✦

To prep for Beijing, I vaccinate, pack host gifts, check garments for holes & tears,

  book a date at the beauty school where a fresh class of

trainees choose names like costume jewelry

  Gwyneth & Eli; Emu & Stella

girls that cut curl & color

  in the mirror I watch a woman

  pluck a cell phone & cash

  from her cleavage

◆

In the desert far from water, a hotel rises from the Gobi

Men in suits & pencil-skirted women

greet guests *Good evening! Good morning!*

*Breakfast is on the roof.*

The view of the Taklamakan as surreal as painted stage sets.

✦

What's not stocked at markets, off-season in May:

winter melon, new year's lanterns, ripened pineapple

Banners touting Olympic tourism canvas streets.

✦

Holidays, war, & packaged events produce Kong Ming candles

   hand-scripted with prayers


wishes on display, I watch
witnesses disengage:

BBQ chefs tend cook-fires,
wait-staff light fuel cells
launching heart-shaped lamps – let go


✦

At midnight a white peony explodes in the sky
cascading waterfalls of magnesium and aluminum light
mark a marriage on the dunes

✦

in a wooden stall for relics
        at Yonghegong Lamasery

glass cases brim with sandalwood
        beads, gemstone rosaries, peach stone coffers

open to reveal buddhas

miniature shrine boxes
    small enough to palm

gold and silver structures

house divinity
        visual displays of religious
                election

*behold, the jewel in the lotus*


strung upon a silver chain: an inlaid prayer locket

✦

love          locked          wedlock

young couples fastening commitment
                                    on the Great Wall shackling

miles of golden padlocks along Ju Yong Guan
                            bought from cultural management
                                    for fifty yuan

keys tossed off
the birth of tourism
in a town called

Lovelock, Nevada
where old women & men
clasp to pets,
small children

✦

this is adaptation:
traditions that constitute
a personal inheritance

what I want to fix more clearly:

the marker of Southern pride
      on the neighbor's patio

stars & bars
          a confederate cross

paired against deep blue
      Asian lanterns,

decorative hangings
            emblazoned with the word "welcome"

enmity cloaked in politesse

the mind turning
      to raise the banner
           of windhorse

# Greenhouse Effect
### AFTER CARSTEN HÖLLER

At the 54th Carnegie International, Carsten Höller installed his *Solandra Greenhouse*. Museum visitors entered a glass-walled chamber filled with *Solandra Maxima* (golden chalice vine), a South American plant that exudes pheromones capable of inducing the hallucinatory effects of falling in love.

five-lobed corolla
blooms deepen
to gold with age

a billet-doux
inscribed on hand-pulled paper
the perfume of golden chalice

a car parked in sunlight
the radiance of two lovers

a vine trained
to grow upwards
can be trapped

take the form
of a box-like hedge,
left untended

a clumped mass

smothering
the native vegetation

the heart's desire
sustained inside

transparent walls

what makes the earth
suitable for life

cultivate enough
to feed a starving nation

# *Hozho*

no

    *words*

        but in

           *actions*

reduce

    compress

present

    tense operations
    perform

bird's eye

    view

           of compost
           composition

           not figure
      against ground

*likeness & unlikeness*

pigment ground
    electrical currents

a basis for
belief in

the collapse of
meaning

into *the intimate* & *the vast*

# The Gathering at the Orchid Pavilion, 2004

cool and dark as
Sensei Nakashima's home
      West Carmen Street
every Monday night
*gakusei* wear wool
sweaters, stockings
beneath ankle-length
skirts gathered neatly
under knees
knelt in tea practice

the cold that penetrates this room
      penetrates the bones
      penetrating still
      the mind

columns you pass between
      tall as stalks in
a bamboo grove

a tickle in the back of the throat
or the heart stirring open

the white-haired docent
      instructs her students,
         *here,*
            *we walk out silently*

# Practice

Pema Norbu Gompo
shares with me a story:
at reaching thirty

thousand prostrations,
glancing into the vanity
to see a trimmed down

waist w/out love
handles – starting over

from zero, more than
once to better
polish his intent

my own practice:
carving holes in
poetry books w/
exacto blade & straight
edge, intervention as
design concept

a hole too uneven
a hole too big
a hole too ragged
a hole too small

every event a mirror
of mind & heart,
imperfect despite
a template for success,
but isn't there
only this work?

day after day
heaps of words piling
up on my writing desk

## Discipline

### FOR SANTI VITAYAUDOM

a grown man
remembers being
a boy of seven

quaking at
the mere mention
of water, his mind

filled with the chime
of ice cream
truck & bicycle

the parched dry of
his own mouth –
an acculturated taste

for water drawn
straight from the tap,
a cloud of slow-rising

bubbles, brimming
liquid settles until
arriving at transparency

a hyper-extended arm &
what your father taught:

hold up this glass

w/out overturning
a drop, & you can set
your sights on anything

## Ironmen

I stand mute when
he shares that the root
of his profession
is to educate,

my healer raced
his last triathalon
for the sake of saying
he competed

some people
can't be schooled even
if all beings are
our teachers –

Pheidippides, that runner
who sped from the battlefield
to Athens, dropped dead
after sprinting twenty-six miles

this gospel the body knows already,
though it's the mind that trains
to steel itself long distance,
screwing up one's courage

## Altar

change comes
whether or not
I hold

true inside
how I see
sometimes

a room/poem/altar
things set in concrete
fixed as though nothing

can ever speak –
the iron-coiled figure
I join to my shrine

a keepsake that asked
for a just memorial,
to mirror *his* place

inside the stone of
my heart the stone
of my heart

## The Diamond Path

the stone of my engagement
ring escapes from its setting
somewhere between

deboarding the plane
at midnight in the Inland
Empire & arriving

at my girlhood home
where the local saying is still
*homicide, suicide, Riverside*

when I wake on the first
day of my stopover,
a yawning loss where light

once winked, the attachments
I've fixed upon in my
misreading of the dharma:

there is always
suffering, something lost;
I grow accomplished

at trading attachments –
a father's affection for a lover's,
the restorative touch of

my naturopath's hands;
I contemplate my wedding
band, remembering this vow:

a circle of gold,
engraved in the Indic script
of Avalokitesvara's mantra,

a promise of recovery
& a dream for the true
wish-fulfilling jewel

## Chop Wood, Carry Water

love and adventure are
words that can be found
in any dictionary -

they are simple days
free of high romance,
excitement another

person might call
them boring:
sweep porch

wash dishes
boil rice
boil water

sit at writing desk
sit before shrine
write poems

I left my work to learn how

sit
sleep
& breathe

I count all the people
who have entered
both my life and

heart on
        one open
                hand

## Lucky

stick after stick
our marriage bamboo
withers, handwritten

wishes slipping
into stink water,

I trim back roots,
& place near light

sponge-like mold
claims yet another
yellow-mottled victim

rehydrate w/ filtered
water, replant
evergreen grafts

we always knew
I wasn't born w/
a natural talent

for nurturing plants,
turn to yarrow
stalks, and sage

advice of i-ching
the unchanging

ground of being,
throwing solid

lines unending,
*perseverance is favorable,*
*progress without blame*

# Chokes

### FOR WHITING TENNIS

I watch him brush
aside thin inedible

fibers, florets from
a thistle blossom

before tasting of
the flower's meat
how I wish I knew

how to handle
the heart of another

firm beneath the tender
pads of tongue &

fingertip, under
rows of thorned

petals piercing
touch the rewards

of digging below choke
to find the disc-like glass

of a clean heart

## Anniversary Poem

at my refuge vow ceremony
my instructor slips me
a white envelope that

I promptly misplace
caught up in the ritual
of rice toss and hair cut

anxiety of arriving to greet
the guru without a silk kata,
the German girl rechristened

Pema offers me her own
& it's her name I really want
but instead I must live with

"liberatress of the Buddha"

inside the card
three square sheets
of recycled paper

stamped with gold
& brushed with orange
familiar to me from

the Chinese grocery –
the aisle my father refused
to travel down, the path

he would not speak of

seven years later,
I rediscover Donna's note
buried in a stack of correspondence

*welcome, dharma sister,*
*welcome* she says again
& I see now the gift

three squares for three jewels
to set fire today to the past
& all its attachments

## Coincident

the healer dies
weeks after giving me
a picture of Jesus

& taking the blue-
green rock of my
ancestral burden

*hand it over,* she said

though I'm far
from Christian, I kept
the grainy xeroxed

copy, a photo
of snowcapped alps,
the image of Christ

in shadowed relief,
I want to believe that
maybe she was ready

to slip away so
quietly just like that
& it wasn't the weight

of a family curse or
hungry ghosts who
stoned an old woman

to death

# Observance
### FOR ROBERT TRAMMELL (1939-2006)

breaths held
for the flyover
of ashes scattering

gathered too late
on the wooden deck
we miss the drop

the blackbirds watching
from telephone lines, the crows
in your poems

tendency to personalize rather than focus on issues; paranoid
rejection of others; rejection of actions –
failure to take something up because rationalize
that I won't be accepted or I won't be CDR, partying
rafting, activities with other people, new games
perfectionism, fear of rejection if not perfect
compulsive
anxious, worries
too much attention to detail, overly plan but still not effective
lack of imagination (now) what happened to dreams
pessimist, defeatist––withdraw if encounters obstacles;
concern over what others think of my
actions or behavior need to be bad
sensitive; easily demoralized;
not a games player;
difficult to recover from attack of my ideas from others;
lack of cleverness; personalize criticism
Lost in self-pity––Mom, Dad, Granny

## Thanatos, Eros

Or,

What happened to dreams?

Too much attention

to detail, failure

to tend to people or

personal encounters

accepting obstacles

recovery from jet

attack, paranoid

worried. A lack

of imagination

but not defeat ––

Mother live lost

not in tissues, not

in self-pity.

## Model Minorities

in the shooter's
face, she recognizes

her sibling's coarse
unforgiving hair,

his yellow skin,
& vacant stare,

the year her brother
broke down, she was

still in high
school, seventeen –

w/ a taste for cutting
not class but hands

& arms any outlet
to escape

this "community"

denies illness,
a family reacts –

against crying out loud
*let it be some other Asian*

in the shooter's
face, I recognize

my sibling's coarse
unforgiving hair,

his yellow skin,
& vacant stare,

the year my brother
broke down, I was

still in high
school,  seventeen –

w/ a taste for cutting
not class but hands

& arms any outlet
to escape

this "community"

denies illness,
a family reacts –

against crying out loud
*let it be some other Asian*

# Requiescat

on campus, co-eds mark
remembrance by wearing
"Free Amanda" shirts,

localizing their support
for the classmate jailed
in Perugia, entangled in

the murder of her flatmate

✦

in the center of Red Square
the flower vigils have stopped
no more bouquets mark the spot

where In Soo Chun doused
himself in gasoline &
set himself on fire

a memory like a burning body
can't be put out with water
bottles/jackets/fire extinguishers

✦

that last week in October,
long after they pronounce him
dead at Harborview,

I hunt for his name
the death of a 61-year-old
immigrant laborer

won't make headline news
unnamed in the *UW Daily*,
I find his identity in *The Stranger*

learn he was assigned
to the Ethnic Studies building
to empty trash baskets

scrub toilets, mop floors
when no one is looking

I lie down to sleep

✦

what part of him failed
out there, the young initiate
who believed what he was

seeing: the death ritual
unfolding before his eyes
contact made

a moment before
cauterized flesh covered
ninety percent of Chun's body

the police made him
stop praying over the corpse
noting him on the record as

a suspected
                    "person of interest"

✦

we save a few
we lose a few

we lose a few too many
we lose a few too many

we lose

## Body Worlds

sideshow with science
at best, grosses over

a billion worldwide
von Hagen's moniker

brands the base of
a woman on bent knees

releasing a dense red
cloud of doves in flight

skin pulled from flesh
to fashion angel wings

the goalkeeper blocks
a soccer ball with one

hand, shows off internal
organs with the other,

dappled grey of smoker's
lung, or just industrial air

pollution? A man parts
the horse's mane in

the second sequence
of tai-chi, hip &

knee joints replaced
with steel, corpses

stolen from mental hospitals
the undocumented bodies

of the executed, bullet holes
found in a specimen's head-

quartered in Dalian & Krygystan

the humanity of bodies stripped
of skin, fatty tissue, age & eye color

a cadaver sliced in two, Hirst's
"mother & child divided,"

chain-sawed parts & not a whole
or was it "two fucking & two

watching" von Hagen's wife
push a rolling pin over what

was once a length of man.
In the educational model

of the body's burden,
I feel the pounding of

my own enlarged heart.

# Thirteen Ways of Looking at a Vulture

eye
of the witness
the I of the commentator


grubby children at the rim
of a Guatemala dump
stunned orphans in Russia


lenses thick
as Coke bottles
motherless boy
in yellowed briefs


finding children
         easier to shoot
because they let
             adults
                 in


mirror compositions: nineteen
guajeros sorting through trash
eighteen vultures foraging

payment to a Third World host family
tendered in Happy Meals

shellshocked
Louisianans housed
at Reunion Arena
survivors – no, *refugees*

Momma Key in curlers
    in the double wide
taxidermied stags and
    an uncle's annual rite
East Texas: guns & boots
    propped against the "I love me" wall

on assignment for
*The New York Times*:
the scorched remains
of the elderly
bus incinerated miles
beyond Dallas

documenting failed
economies amusement
parks crushed by Disney

nineteen vultures
to be located within the frame
eighteen visible, and one unseen


*Under 25*, years in
which the artist modeled
shit-filled napkins –
Nan Goldin already
shooting junkies


empty love
hotel rooms
        "pregnant,"
         with "meaning"

## Corps de Ballet

within a wooden frame
a sequence of lobsters scuttle

     from kitchen to parlor
     trading the ocean's deeps
     for the depths of a smackman's p(l)ot

         lured by the perfume
         of herring & live bait

lobstermen haul
     boxes aboard
         throwing star
            fish scattered in
all directions
     undersized specimens rejected
         at the weigh-in

         trapped in beaded necklaces
            and netted skirts
               pincers rubber banded
                  tight, the taping
            of a ballerina's feet
        measured lengths of silk cord

wrapping

a line of boiled red crustaceans          swimmerets spread

                    teasing the taste buds     towards
                    another course

# Metaphysique d'ephemera

### AFTER JOSEPH CORNELL

a pantry
ballet  for
Jacques
Offenbach

ECHAPPE´
EN RELEVE
SOUS-SUS
ALLONGE´
MENU TENDU
SAUTE´

*ceci*

*n'est pas*

*une*

*ecrivisse*

demitasse
caviar
absinthe
bouillon
silver
spoon
washboard
& jug

tossed
salad
a la
russe

## Sugar Daddy

refined & white
a man made of artificial

sweetener sugar
cubed, a young girl's

longing for something
other than Equal

every kiss, jawbreaker
brittle lollipop – love that rots

teeth, leaves you
w/ diabetes, obesity

the sticky saccharine
of what the body

can't resist craving –
melting in your mouthfeel

## La Quinta del Sordo

in the *villa*
*of the deaf man*
fourteen frescoes
painted al secco
after near-death
experience,
the silence of
a sectarian chapel
hung with coal dark
triptychs & panels
the rectangle
of an exit portal
cut away
to black

## Spring Peepers, Summer Flowering


invisible singers

                                                              awaken from winter

slumber under logs,

                      loose bark

at the edge                               of bodies

                      of water

                      sounding courtship songs

                              my father and I

                              share a memory of

                              staying awake to witness

the night-blooming cereus

                              white queen flower

a balm for the heart

blooms in the backyard

just once before withering

# Bell(e)

AFTER TOSHIKO TAKAEZU

in centuries
past, sunk
beneath soil

to draw earth's
vital force, inert
vessel of

sound + light,
conserved

in a museum
of curative plants
the moment of

stillness &
gathering before
the shudder

of first sound

dreaming
the shake of chime,
hum &

g o n g

# Dropping Through El Dorado Gap

## Autumn Nijuin Renga with Andrew Schelling

autumn foliage scorches
the horizon line forest
fires in Esperanza

    in the withered tomato garden
    recalling his aged mother's voice

contemplating sameness
the artist silkscreens one
more canister of soup

    moon on a previous canvas
    had trapped some wolf-like passion

sleep disturbed by dream
the body recalls roughness
of tongue against skin

    once in a high summer grass
    a heifer lapped salt from his shoulder

she pulls onto
a gravel roadside to scrape
moths from her windshield

    hesitant hand on roadmap
    name of each town portentous

Blanket, Early, Venus
Big Lake, signs on the path
to the wild old West

  the evening star hurts him
  dropping through El Dorado gap

fragrant hair
resinous as Great Basin sage
spooky all night frost dreams

  rain turning overnight to ice
  she slips & loses her footing

moon high on the Ganges
a sickle on each
frozen hair blade

  damaged cells in the bloodstream
  the body slowly shutting down

aching, chattering,
under blankets all night –
dawn brings a winter eagle

  shoulder blades pulled wide in
  garuda, the spine elongating

or so it seems —
rhododendrons break out across
your flanks, o spring peaks

    this evergreen, honey of Asia
    Minor gives rise to reverie

how it cuts
the first year's violet petal
touching his entrails

    sky bursting with wetness
    the heart split wide again

# At the Roadside Lumberyard

## Winter Nijuin Renga with Andrew Schelling

Torn cloud and snow
blown across high glacial rock –
then note of a lone horn

        in winter bands of ewes
        roaming alpine valleys

even in cities
their tender hooves soothe me
past taxis, frozen slush, hard moon

        a cab driver returns a sack of
        diamonds left in a trunk

in my heart
love's bright facets, though rain's
washed out the love poem

        tired sonnets & lackluster odes fall
        short of summer showers' beauty

the road of poetry
is dark, bitter, & solitary –
Hah-hah!

prizing a shared connection
we send tidings across the currents


this morning I see
"the person you were born"
singing with a blurred left eye

        bird song on waking, the body takes
        in its first glass of distilled water

drinking the air
of North America after
a long journey East

        he recalls October apricots
        drying near the army cantonment

in the valley of Cashmere
Turkish lokum poured from
autumn harvest

        we call it Full Corn Moon
        respite from a nation at war

keeping an ear to
earth, cold words of global
warming, polar caps & bear

wild fire, bark beetle
spreading north to Alaska's tundra

at a roadside lumberyard
piles of cut logs squared
stacks of two-by-fours

ah, ancestors –
the Siouxland cottonwood's tiny buds

there on NCAR mesa
 a flowering prickly pear
she laughs & weeps for her father

the drum of woodland flame
hammering out its heart

# Moonviewing

on the night of the last
lunar eclipse, moon's
alignment moves into

earth's outline, to be over-
shadowed by the brightness
of headlight, brakelight,

blinking red stoplight;
this ink dark dome marked
by floodlight & helicopter

washes out buildings
in Roosevelt Square glaring
from Sleep Country to

Dream Clinic, I desert
to Greenlake, where mirage-like
this necklace of lamplight

encircles the reservoir
misled by grinning cobrahead
diffusers flattening into

a florescent skyscape,
why give another thought to
an old poet moon

# Beneath the Word Oneness
## FOR GAO PING

While divining *The American Heritage Dictionary*, my finger
lands upon the entry for ONE-NIGHT STAND, [*noun:* a one
time encounter between paramours], indexed below the word
ONENESS. Might their close proximity in the English lexicon
suggest some connection, that oneness, a condition of being
undivided, can be brought about through the ephemerality of
sexual intimacy limited to chance occasion?

Earlier that day, my friend visits me in my studio and we share
a picnic lunch from the colony kitchen: fried potstickers, raw
celery, and clear soup. A thermos spills on the deck and slivers of
green onion stick to wood. We save the fortune cookies for last.
The message on his slip of paper reads, "ASK THAT SPECIAL
SOMEONE OUT ON A DATE SOON."

Perhaps it is best explained in terms of an analogy to food. Take
for instance, *Shui Zhu Niu Rou*, "water boiled beef," Szechuan
style cuisine, a specialty from the South. Maybe the dish looks
right, delicate cuts of prime beef, carefully prepared. Sauce glazed,
piquant. The flavor is even okay. But, how it feels in the body
somehow *wrong*. Unfamiliar as an unwanted kiss, sloppy, with
too much tongue, poor substitute for the real thing. Compare this
to the same meal made for you by your lover, ingredients bought
fresh from the night market, the right balance of every dish served
up to you, steaming, in every moment a familiarity and tenderness
welcome in your mouth as the touch and taste of first love.

## We'll Always Have Cheyenne

FOR PHILLIP BARNHART

along for the adventure

an impromptu trip
across state lines

to taste the free range,
of hamburgers grown

where grass is greener,

our rental runs low
on gas – only

enough fuel to
get us half

the way back
in a borrowed car

we could travel no
further than that

# A Day Without an Immigrant, Dallas, Texas

At Pearl Street station,
two brown-skinned men

in painter's pants stand
out in a sea of white

I am just one more face
sticking out in a crowd

& it is my privilege

that prevents me from
understanding why

the workers want to know
how to buy one-way trips

the automated machine
sells only one roundtrip fee,

back to where you came from

he isn't asking me for change
says it clear enough so that

there can be no mistake
*Sí. Yo sé.*

*But a dollar fifty is a lot of money.*

# Watching My Father Crush a Black Widow
## on My Last Day in California

when the laborer
fell through on finishing
the job, my father

left the trunk
to dry on the front
lawn, eighty pounds

of amputated wood
to hack away at
slowly – when I

see him walk
outside, machete
in one hand &

log in the other
I follow, sensing
there will be violence –

maybe a dismembered
finger, or wood
chip to the eye –

he orders me to
heap sticks &
leaves in the yard

waste receptacle
where I discover
the black widow

upside down,
a red hourglass
marking

her abdomen,
the insect we were
all conditioned

to fear, as children,
a mature specimen
in webbed suspension

is hard to ignore
but I do, piling
wood around her

habitat; my father
tells me to kill it
with a stick &

when I keep stacking
saying silent mantras
to will the widow away,

he breaks a bough &
stabs until he's pinned her
to the plastic wall

I watched how
she never fought
back & then I

covered her body
beneath a mountain
of dead branches;

around us, life
grows wild – algae
blooms in the swimming pool

weeds sprout
through concrete,
mold colonizes a roof

dried lilies in the sunburnt
koi pond, gophers tearing
up the lawn that

my father cuts back
with the rusted mower
blades dulled by

sticks & wood
he intends to bury
beneath the ground

once all life has
drained away
beyond any

possibility of
regeneration –
I think of

the stump that
is my older brother,
the mother that

escaped w/ her life,
the girl that grew up
dreading spiders

learning that
either we kill
or be killed

### Search & Recovery

for James Kim (1971 – 2006)


it could have
happened to any
of us

a wrong turn
down a logging road
tires tunneled
into snow

a man's undying
love for his children

moves satellites
maps aerial images

eighteen care packages
dropped over 16
miles of the Siskiyou,

bearing handwritten
notes from a father
to his son

the signs
you left for those
who came after you

a red t-shirt
a wool sock,
a child's blue skirt

layers of a life,
stripped down to
a family's fate –

the weight of being
unseen – to travel
a path back to

what you knew
at birth, the warmth
of being held close

brought home

## Double Happiness

ON THE OCCASION OF BAO XISHUN'S WEDDING
AND KIM BONG-SEOK'S REUNION WITH HIS FATHER

the tallest man in the world
reaches into the gullet of
an ailing dolphin to retrieve
undigested bits of plastic

human hands more
sensitive than any
surgical instrument

after 55 years
of wifelessness,
his mother in the ground
marriage circulars dispatched to
the far corners of the earth,

chooses a bride
from Chifeng
his hometown,
what's nearest to
the human heart.

A boy separated
from his parents
on the streets of Pusan
grows up on the slopes
of Vail to win

bronze at Turin, prizes
more dearly
the journey of
reaching outward
to find a way home
to this body, his birth
father, this motherland

# Notes

21 Retort
You Guoying is a Chinese migrant worker from southwestern Sichuan province who suffered a brain hemorrhage and was nearly cremated alive. Her family deposited her at a crematorium in Taizhou, because they could no longer afford her hospital treatments.

In the crematory trade, the retort is a chamber where a body is placed for incineration.

44 Hozho
The title of the poem references the Navajo word for beauty, balance, harmony – "and the effort towards."

62 Coincidence
I consulted with an energetic healer that specialized in working with ancestral wounds and intergenerational trauma. I went to see the healer once, and before I could schedule another session, I learned that she had died abruptly of a brain aneurysm in her sleep.

64 Observance
Robert Trammell was Dallas' best-known outsider poet. Publisher of Barn Burner Press and founder of the literary nonprofit, WordSpace, which endures today, Robert was an important poetic elder. Of his dozens of books, Birds remains a favorite.

66 Thanatos, Eros
The source text of "Thanatos, Eros" is transcribed directly from an artifact held in the collections of the Suho Memorial Paper Museum, Taipei, Taiwan.

69 Requiescat
In 2007, Amanda Knox, an undergraduate student at the University of Washington, was implicated in the murder of her flatmate, Meredith Kercher, while the two participated on a study abroad program in Italy.

The murder attracted a large amount of attention in Seattle and remains a source of media frenzy.

In contrast, the death of In Soo Chun, an immigrant laborer terminated from his position at the University of Washington, received scarcely any news coverage, though dozens of students on campus witnessed the violence of Chun's self-immolation.

81 METAPHYSIQUE D'EPHEMERA

The poem is a response to Joseph Cornell's *A Pantry Ballet for Jacques Offenbach* – a box of dancing lobsters. The diorama pays homage to the French composer who wrote *Les Contes d'Hoffmann*.

Cornell used the term *metaphysique d'ephemera* to describe the quality of "everyday magic." The original term is attributed to poet Gerard de Nerval.

87 DROPPING THROUGH EL DORADO SPRINGS: AUTUMN NIJUIN RENGA

Renga is a collaboratively authored form of linked poetic verse that originated in ancient Japan. Andrew Schelling and I passed poetic stanzas back and forth over mail and email, guided by detailed schemas that specified syllable count, stanza structure, images, seasons, and mood. We alternated between 3- and 2-line stanzas, occasionally breaking with pattern to allow enough freedom to extend an image or thought.

90 AT THE ROADSIDE LUMBERYARD: WINTER NIJUIN RENGA

While "Dropping through El Dorado Springs" was written between Boulder, CO, and Dallas, TX, the verses in "At the Roadside Lumberyard" were exchanged between India and the Pacific Northwest.

102 SEARCH & RECOVERY

James Kim was trapped in the southwestern Oregon backcountry with his wife and two young children, when his family's station wagon became stranded in deep snow. Kim left the car in search for help and never returned. His wife and children were rescued.

Shin Yu Pai is the author of *Haiku Not Bombs* (Booklyn Artists Alliance), *Works on Paper* (Convivio Bookworks), *Sightings: Selected Works, 2000–2005* (1913 Press), *The Love Hotel Poems* (Press Lorentz), *Unnecessary Roughness* (xPress(ed)), *Equivalence* (La Alameda Press), and *Ten Thousand Miles of Mountains and Rivers* (Third Ear Books). Her work is anthologized in *The Wisdom Anthology of North American Buddhist Poetry* and *America Zen: A Gathering of Poets*, as well as *City Visible: Chicago Poetry for the Next Century* and *For the Time Being: The Bootstrap Book of Poetic Journals*. Shin Yu received her MFA from the School of the Art Institute of Chicago and studied at Naropa University. She has completed residencies at Taipei Artist Village, the MacDowell Colony, the Ragdale Foundation, and was one of five inaugural fellows to participate in the Life of Discovery Fellowship Program sponsored by the International Writing Program at the University of Iowa. She is former assistant curator for The Wittliff Collections and has taught creative writing at Southern Methodist University and the University of Texas at Dallas. Presently, she lives in Conway, Arkansas, where she directs the Hendrix-Murphy programs in literature and language at Hendrix College.